Quadrantaria.

J. Ray

*D_E_L_E_T_E_*.

It'll hit me

When I'm all alone in my dorm

With the lights out

And the silent yet deafening pitter-patter

Of rain bouncing off my window

Catches my attention through the light of the moon's

Last kiss that I…

Would give anything for some company.

Lonely.

A wide smile

Curls the ends of her

Lips as she creeps closer and closer

To the new born boy

And ends his life

With her fatal kiss goodnight.

Shadow.

You are as fake as they come

Once you drive all your friends away

With your lies and your knives in their backs

You'll have no one left to gossip to

You'll be all alone with your thoughts wondering

Where it all went wrong,

I can promise you after all you've done to us

We are never coming back.

Dagger.

I am disgusted in myself

For ever thinking I saw something

Other than hate in you,

You are the destroyer

But I am the survivor.

Odi Et Amo.

What more do you want me to say?

Congratulations?

Thank you?

You ruined all the parts of me that I ever cherished

I hope you have fun with my heart.

Fragile.

She barks out orders with promises of a joy

So grand, so rejuvenating

That it simply does not exist.

ERROR.

Don't let her looks deceive you

Underneath that sheet so brilliant is a monster

A monster whose only goal is snatching you up

Taking your life

One

Breath

At a time.

Onyx.

It's funny how you think you have the authority

To tell me what I do and don't deserve.

Suffrage.

All the time we feel like caged animals

Ready to unleash love and devotion

On our owners like the obedient little puppies we are

While our masters see us as nothing but wolves

Wolves with the taste of blood and plight on our
tongues,

They will not embrace us.

They will not protect us.

They will only euthanize us.

Humane.

What hurts the most

Is how you believe I'm anything at all like him

The one who made you this way

I hope you realize that it's not me who has become him

It's you.

Reversal.

She took everything and left me with

The feelings of being nothing

The feelings of being unloved

The feelings of being too little

And it burns holes in my head

All I can utter is how much it hurts.

It hurts so bad

The pain is worse than that of broken bones or torn
muscles.

It hurts so bad

Knowing you'll never be enough for her.

Enough.

You're hideous

The way you hide behind that screen of yours

Playing puppet master

Pulling strings of texts

Words meant to bait your prey

Luring him in with falsehoods

Flirty but malevolent you tease

Utilizing this poor boy into doing your every bidding

He cares for you and you abuse that

His eyes are sealed shut by your ruse

Send him those hearts

Send him those pictures

Send him those promises

Then flake on him like you always do.

Simulacrum.

It's easy to find yourself caring

For people who don't give a damn about the real you.

Looking back into what could only be described

As a living hell,

The actions- the speech

All of it I was so fortunate to receive from you

Revealing to my eyes the Face of Vanity

Yet being blind enough by a lustful attraction

Kept my mind from processing the validity of it...

The painfully obvious truth that in your heart

There lies only room for one, you

Conceited, selfish, narcissistic you.

Narcissus.

I fought back all the monsters just to find out that the real evil

Was the one I spent my life protecting.

Snow.

You've got a war inside you

Buried six feet deep

Killing you ever so slowly

Drip by drip

Blood by blood

Leaving the enemy woundless

Leaving the enemy victorious.

Self-Inflicted.

You've become my fucking god

But you show zero mercy instead you hate

It's sentient enough to crawl out of your heart

And roam the halls of Hades' Palace

It's void like eyes stare me down

Helping me come to the realization that I must defy
you

I must overthrow

Topple your pedestal

Stand up to you, face to face and become

The master of my own kingdom.

Nice Guys.

It hurts knowing how little I cross your mind

How you are so preoccupied and oblivious to my feelings

How you'll never see me as more than just the one

The one who keeps you from boredom.

Toy.

After all this time,

You taught me to hate you

Instead of love you.

Juxtaputopia.

I'm sorry for everything we've ever said

Or ever done

Not said

Or not done

For loving you like I did

For caring for you…like I did

I'm sorry we ever met that day

The heat of the summer

I'm sorry I locked eyes with you

And in that moment, fell harder than Achilles

I'm sorry that we talked

I'm sorry that we danced

I'm sorry that we loved

I wish I could make it up to you

Wipe our heads clean of the memories

You know I'm sorry right?

Sorry for everything.

Gods.

There is no hope of resurrecting the dead weight we carry

The truth is it is only a bug in an infinite loop program.

Python.

You can talk about wanting to do shit with me all you
want

Because I know the truth

The truth is you'll just stay in your house all week

Doing nothing but tormenting me with lies

Through texts and expect me not to realize

How little interest you have

And how clearly

I am just a tool for your attention.

Flake.

Even in my dreams you find a way to upset me.

One of the worst things you do to me

Is open that deceptive little mouth of yours

Anything can happen in ten years

Who knows where you and I will be

It's difficult for you to utter the words

There is no more

And if you can't believe that now

What the fuck is going to happen in ten years

That would ever change your stubborn head.

Malignant.

The same pictures in which I'd stop and stare

Filling my heart with butterflies, blood pumping, eyes dilating

Dreams of long lost lovers

They now scar my vision

The initial response is to reach in

Tear my eyes from the figures frozen on screen

Nausea sets in rapidly fighting alongside his brother Coma

As my body begins to feel a sick and twisted abomination of hatred

Loss

Sadness

It penetrates my very life essence

It's as if looking at these pictures makes my blood boil

My heart slow

Life to cease

If only for a second.

DEL.

I miss you and I want to see you

But it's probably best we don't.

Contradictions.

You know as much as I do that nothing you send her

As good, pure, or lovely as it may sound

Is going to make a goddamn difference to her

So that text you've been wanting to send

The one you keep retyping

The one explaining how done you are with this shit

It really isn't worth the thought

So instead of thinking of sending that

Let her have it

Tell her how you really feel

Just say what's on your mind.

Advice.

Drugged internally.

If you're trying to teach me a lesson

I get it ok

You don't have to go out of your way

To torment and torture me just because

I was the unfortunate fool who fell so deeply in love
with you

I get it

I do.

Everything Dilemma.

To think I was the only one

Who ever gave a damn about you

I hope it burns you up knowing no one

Could ever compare to my love

And when you've scorched yourself here on earth

Off to blaze in the presence of your second death

In the realm of the fiery furnace you are so
accustomed to.

Damned.

It still blows my mind

How a single person

Can make you feel every emotion known to exist

In such as short window of time.

Rollercoasters.

I'll never understand what I did

To deserve the pain you brought upon me

I fucking loved you

That's all I ever did.

Payback.

I awoke alone in a crypt

Tattered, with slits on my wrists

The well of blood offered to the beast

Had run dry and began to crust over the layers

The leftover skin was brittle

Loneliness consumed my every thought

Deceived by the creature

Placed into a hollow prison

Manipulated into trading blood for company

The thief stole my heart, locked me away

She feasted on her meal in privacy

The monster as I recall stood tall

Blackened-blue eyes that melted my mind

As I stared into the abyss of her bluff

Which was an amalgamation of both beauty and
villainy

Her hair luscious yet provoking instilling in me

Dreams of golden rivers and heavenly plains

She fueled my desire by a lightness in touch

Stimulating the lesser parts of man

All these- lies, lies, lies

My forsaken heart so lost for partnership

Blind by true craving

Gave into her prerequisites of love

And in giving all the life essence away

I have been denounced to nothing

I exist only in a plane of suffrage

The emotion, love, was stolen from me in falsehood

Replaced by a cavern of emptiness

Distortion, manipulation, hatred leak from the walls

So violet the cracks in this prison

The coarse graying floor is a cage

There is no hallucinating this

THIS IS REALITY

Compelling tears to stream down my face

And echo the sound of isolation through the crypt

The crypt of my heart's pilferer.

Isolationism.

It's incredibly hard trying to justify some of the
choices

Especially the bullet to my brain

Which I unloaded on myself

This day in history.

9/10.

You tell me

Don't you dare shed one more tear

But the taste of salt from the millions you left me
with

Burns my tongue and scars my throat even still.

Tears.

I've grown immune to your poisonous kiss.

Believed I could've lived a perfectly happy, joyous life

Spending each living moment on your heels

Like a dog,

I count my blessings ever night

Thanking God in the highest

For freeing this poor ol' pup.

Hydrants.

Oh how it burns and cuts into my heart

To be captivated by a beauty

Whose love has been taken

I must remove myself from this place

The feelings will become stronger

Become sentient

Controlling my beliefs and actions,

I will live in everlasting pain if I fail

To remove myself from your company.

Wasteland.

Brittle is your love

So difficult to maintain

Sharp and jagged

It cuts into me, shattering like glass

Leaving remnants buried deep in my blood

Circulating my body

Surrendering that lasting gash, forever part of me.

Rustic.

Constantly teasing me with satisfaction

Yet you deliver nothing to my tongue

And I'm cursed to witness your beauty

In and out of my haunted head as nightmares

That corrode my very perceptions,

They dance along the floor

They stay lurking under my bedsheets

I'd kill for you

I'd KILL for you

Just give up, lower the walls of your heart

Withholding your love

Give up, lower the walls

Make me as royal as King or Queen in your palace

Forget these games, let me in and I'll erase the pain

Let it happen…us in love.

Bait.

I pity the unfortunate soul who ends up

finding you next.

She broke me

That's what she did

She took the whole thing

Smashed it to fucking bits.

10/22.

I think it's time to address the problem,

I was so willing to look past all your flaws

And turn away when you sinned against me

I showed you kindness and love

I imagined that'd be enough to change you

Make you see the light
Make you feel whole

But I guess that's the thing right,

I tried everything to love you

And everything to help you that it finally occurred to me

That you did not deserve anything I offered you

And that I will gladly find my other half elsewhere.

Enlightenment.

You filled me with lies

You drained me to dust.

Quadrantaria.

Moved on

She's already moved on

Forgotten all about me and all I've done

Part of me knew she never felt the same

That's why she ran to him

She just keep me warming the benches.

Field.

If you want a promise I'll give you this:

I promise

I promise I'll never let another you

Into my life again.

Promises.

I'll be sure you lose everything and everyone

Anyone you've ever wronged

Because the more you harm me

The more powerful my words become

And the more powerful I become the more afraid you
are

I'll destroy everything you know

The same as you have done to me

And my words will become whistleblowers

My warnings will shape spears

Each of which will ruin and topple you

If you begin to wonder what went wrong

Know you caused it all

When you sought out to stab me in the back

Just like you have done to everyone else.

Matthew.

She deserves so much better than a man with a pen

She deserves a man with a sword.

Mighty.

When they regret all they've done to you

Remember how unapologetic

How destructive

How malicious

And unrelenting they were when they kicked you out

Without even a second thought.

Homecoming.

Alas the sky opened up and began to weep

For it has seen this detriment before.

Climate Change.

The overwhelming fear that engulfs my body

As I debate whether I should text you

Really puts our whole relationship in perspective.

Read.

I'm so afraid

I'm so afraid

The thought of losing you

It plagues my mind, dilutes my blood

It's all I can think about

It hurts so much coursing through my head

It hurts so much

You are my light and my everything

The world can not offer me anything over you

Only you, you can offer me the world

And I love you for that

But I'm afraid and this is my confession:

What if you don't love me back, the way I love you
oh so much?

What if you find someone better?

What if I pull us apart with my mistakes or all my
problems?

What if I hold too tightly like I often do?

These thoughts, these concerns

A cloud raining acid on my mind hanging above me
everyday

Leaving me so afraid- baby, I'm so afraid.

Fear.

I will not allow you to torture me

Drag me down the broken path

With a dark woodland scene approaching

To hang me by my head

Then cut me apart piece by piece

No, I will not return to those woods

Never again.

Two.

It feels as if everything I've ever loved

Has been ripped from my skin...

I can no longer feel

No longer cry

No longer live.

NO LONGER

NO LONGER

NO LONGER

NO LONGER

  NO LONGER

NO LONGER

 NO LONGER

NO LONGER

                     NO LONGER

NO LONGER

                                    NO LONGER

  NO LONGER

                                    NO NONO LONGE

R

NO LONGER

                                    NO LONGE

R

NO LONGER

                                  NO LONGER

NO LONGER

                                    NO LO

N GER NO LONGER LLLLLLOO   *N*

OLONNNGER   *NO LONGER*

NO LONGER

                                  NO LONGERRR

She's indecisive because she's afraid of failing

She has been through it all before

And has developed fear for her future

She is branded by a hell that consumed her once before

I wish I could silence her stress

I'm nothing like her past but she has no clue…

She means everything to me

And I'm dying

Because she's afraid of who I am.

Afraid.

All the signs of your hate

All the signs of your abuse

The manipulation

The attention you seek out in others

The way you profit from us

Use us

All the signs of your true colors

And I choose to give you a chance.

Signs.

Amazing the damage delivered in only one year of existence

How it can be so devastating

How it ends up written in stone for the rest of eternity.

1692-1693.

From the moment we met

To the moment we parted ways

All I saw was through tunnel vision,

I was blind,

My head filled with only her and her service

But I can finally say with the sole intention of being
honest

That peace can only be found if you cut off your
bloodsucker

I've been released

And now I see how stupid I was to allow you my life,

I would gladly walk through Hell

Than ever see your face once more.

Pax Romana.

On the other side

Where the light meets an end

The dirt turns quickly to leeching swamps

To rainfall from above- acidic

It bubbles my skin to ash

Smells of decaying flesh fill my ever-draining senses,

God I miss your radiant light

I miss your lovely smile,

You cast me out into the darkness

To fight on my own

Forever chasing the ghost of you.

Committed.

Moved past my butterflies

This passion that burns for you

Invisible as you love him instead.

Burner.

She is so gorgeous

A prismatic beauty projecting dreams

Of never ending sunsets and hand holding eternity

That leaves me awestruck by her rosy and violet aura

A twilight delight

The only candy to my eyes

Sweet, satisfying, and delicious

Yet that is all she is…a view

A monument to my heart

I am nothing more to her than a sidekick or perhaps
the other guy

The best friend or a friend at best

She sees me not as more

And it hurts like stabs puncturing my mind, body, and soul

I see her

This rainbow in a dark and dreary life

A visual breathtaking

But she can not be held by a man like me

Her pot of gold belongs to someone else.

Zipped Jacket.

She's out there...she's just not me.

I honestly don't care how much you overanalyzed us

It's fucking clear

I get it

You could never love me back

But I'll never in a million years be able to sit here

Keys clicking

And say I know you care about me

Like you swear you fucking do,

If you cared the slightest bit you would have let me go

Or given us the chance a million years ago.

Mil.

You could make any situation

Seem like everyone else's fault

And you'd always play victim.

Spin Doctor.

Being so far away from her

Yet feeling her presence even still

Like a magnet she draws me in

Her new toy

The one she teases

Knowing no limitations on distance

She imagines her beauty miles away

While also occupying herself with another man

But I am as loyal as they come

And maybe one day she will notice this

Maybe one day she will treat her toy with love and
devotion

The kind of relationship he certainly deserves.

Miles.

Left trying for a girl who could not even feel his

presence.

Our minds can become enemies

Our control becomes relinquished

They put up a simulation of what is real

What is unreal

The simulation in my head, it targeted you

Told me *she's perfection*

When this cloak came undone

The illusion was eradicated

And when I opened my eyes

I was staring not into perfection

I was staring into the eyes of an attention whore.

Grid.

Stuck in a trance

The beauty of her petals

Draws me in closer to her thorns of anguish.

Rosy.

It's not easy seeing her with him in the mirrors of our world

Projected to me from the comfort of my home

Or rather the discomfort

Once I eye my precious little girl holding that boy so tightly

As if she as no options left,

It burns within me like a molten core

Stains my eyes with tar and ash

I'm hollow inside simply because

He is hers and she is his

Every time I'm cursed to see them together

I recognize that I am nothing but a watchman in their lives

Withering away layer by layer to muscle and bone...

She would be much happier

I would be much happier

In a life without him

But as much as I hold onto this belief

As much as I crave this reality

I am nothing but late, late in the presence of her beautiful.

Late.

We are friends. That's all we are, all we were, and all

we ever will be.

You're not secretive

They way you ignore my texts

But believe I'm so naïve to accept that you're just always busy.

Haunt.

The constrictor coiled itself around my heart

Squeezing, clinging, choking the flow of love

Restricting me from kissing the lips of my dearest

These tendrils of suffocation

Contort my vessels from breath

They clog and shackle my soul till I was silent

Forevermore.

Win.

Your only job was to give her a reason

To wake up each morning

But instead

You gave her a reason to give up every night.

Priorities.

Oh how I wish to be yours

Like a star soaring in the midnight sky

I repeat this dream of us

What it would taste like knowing our feelings are real

A reality ripe for the taking

An assimilation of our love manifesting our new
destiny as one

Alas you are afraid

Taken in

Blinded by another

He leeches off our inevitability

This substitution instead of adaption of your new life

Your time with him rots and curbs the fruit of us

The life as one…

Is again fantasy at most.

Another.

You taught me how to become nothing

From something

And I just want it all back.

Learned.

When you love them so much

But can no longer make them smile

There is no worse feeling.

Happy.

This is what you've done to me

You've taken it all

Even my will to write about how disgusting you are

It's all gone

And I don't know what to do,

You act like you payed me a favor

Like you somehow did the right thing

You dragged me through hell

Then let go of me after I was short of your desires,

Whether you like to admit it or not

I was too much for you

It scared you

The boundless limitations of my love

The lengths I would go for you

All you could see in me was a mess

And I was never your definition of perfect,

I think the sad truth is that I tried

I changed every possible detail of my life for you

Ones you wouldn't even see with the naked eye

I could have been anything you fucking wanted

I was yours, but you refused me…

Why?

What did I do to you to make you hate me?

God, I put everything into you and you couldn't even

toss me a fucking bone

What did I do to deserve this treatment?

I played your sick game

I played it to down to the last move

And even when I thought you'd finally let me win

You pulled it out from under me,

Now I'm here, up at fucking two o'clock

Typing out who knows what…when really there is no

point

It's all meaningless, you finally got your victory

You destroyed me

I hope you're happy knowing you took a man

A pure hearted man full of happiness and grace

You took that man

The one with all the potential in the world

You took that fucking man

And smashed him, crushed him, collapsed him into

nothing

You turned him into fucking nothing,

After all he did for you

The worst part of it all is he can't even fucking hate

you

You won't even let him have that.

Best Day Ever.

Waiting for the orders, to execute ourselves.

Now that you can see

Look at all the desolation when under her spell

She disguised it like sunshine and lollipops.

Illusionary.

I hope you enjoy the rest of your day

That's what I tell her

As she goes off to spend time with another man

One who doesn't deserve her.

Mud.

Here's hoping she'll come around

Late at night

Eyes moistening to the thought of you

Realizing how empty she is without you

Realizing what happiness you gave her

Realizing…

I guess that's what happens

They take for granted what's wonderful

And when it's gone

They beg and plead

They pray for its glorious return.

Figure It Out.

If you are reading this

Know I haven't forgotten

I will never forget.

Tombstone.

I can't erase it from my head

It plays like a movie

Over and over and over and over and over and over and over and over and over and over

Over and over and over and over and over and over and over and over and over and over

I see you with him, it's so vivid

Hot, sweaty, and sticky

The sounds you make, the calling of more

Eyes rolling to the back of your head

The curvature of spines

The initial push to reactive pull

Hands flying freely, and you grip him

He grabs those beautiful pieces of you

And in receiving this pleasure, this complete
envelopment of love

It kills me
KILLS ME

Every blow
Every scream
Every name
Every mix of you and him in sweat, blood, and worse

KILLS ME

He'll always have that over me

No matter what

He'll always own that part of you

And how can I ever live up to that.

Suppress.

Jumping rope in the school yard ended up tying

nooses in our hearts.

You make it so difficult to say the truth,

Tell me what's on your mind dear

Tell me, if you never want to see me again just say so

I'll grant you that wish.

Genie.

Her whole life is filled with lies

Spun into her psychotic web to the point where

Even her breaths are artificial.

Web.

Just type

That's what I tell myself when I'm thinking of all the ways

To copy down the disgust you put me through,

To make use of all these dreary thoughts in my head

Just type

And it'll all come out eventually.

Keyboard.

We were never on the same page

I think that was our problem all along.

400th.

I'm going to reinforce what I'm sure you already know by now

That what you did to us

Was, how'd you put it?

The worst decision of them all.

And I hope you feel that every waking moment

Of everyday and every night

When you look to your ex

When you look to your friends

When you look to the neighbors at your door

And all of them are so fucking happy

And all of them are so in love

And there you are

All alone, crying

107

Crying because everyone you know

Crossed you up and found someone so much better than you

Everyone moved on from you

Let that sink in
Let it sting like it stung for me when you threw me away
Let it bubble your skin
Let it cause your agony
Let those tears fall like acid

Down that beautiful heartbroken face

You choose this remember?

The worst decision of them all.

XOXO.

I speak in wrecking balls

Demolishing the palace I built

The walls of diamond and halls of gold

They will all collapse to my words

Just as you will collapse and crumble

To your hands and knees

Begging for forgiveness.

Weeks.

There for you

I was always there for you,

Giving you everything both physical and emotional

I handed it all to you

Crying over the keys on my keyboard

Wanting to erase you so much

Everything I had done for a witch like you

The time wasted trying to please you

Addicted to the belief that I could somehow satisfy
you

Physically, emotionally- it doesn't matter

That was all I ever wanted

To kiss at your heels

Faking your gratification when I gave you everything

Knowing that nothing would ever be good enough.

Hugs.

These nights will never be the same

Instead of dreaming us together

I'll be awake, living us apart.

10/21.

She lets you down, abuses your devotion,

and chains you up.

Don't you see?

You can't play the lover and the friend

If you want friendship, I'll give you the boy

Don't be surprised when he is nothing

Like the man that reeled you in.

Choice.

It's a curse

Feeling unrequited love

Being so sure you've found the one

Really it's just a trick your eyes play on your heart.

Kids.

It's cold, dark, and a shiver crawls up my leg

Sliding, slitting my back to blood

I'm so alone

It stings

These tears roll from my eyes and nothing is worse

Than watching this body decay night after night

It stares me dead in the face

As if the first words were stuck between chasms of teeth

All raw and sweaty

The scars are permanently etched in skin...

I was late

So very late

If only I was quicker

If only I had been different

If only

If only

What's done is done

The wounds cannot be erased

The moment will be eternalized

I was not even conceived at this point

I was slow, but also far from the action

My only option now is to accept the loss

Move on

There is no time to grieve.

Known.

It's a constant fear in my head

Like I'll never be good enough for you

I'm afraid of losing you so much

You'll see the burden I really am, and you'll run

Who can blame you?
Let's just hope you leave before it gets too serious.

Anything.

It's one A.M. and she has no clue how I lie here

Staring at the wall

Beating my pillow to death with tears barreling down
my face

Like expanding snowballs

How I'm dying inside

How it hurts so much to be so far away from you

The pain of waking up everyday in a world nowhere
near you

Nowhere near my love

It's bullshit,

EVERY

SINGLE

FUCKING

DAY

How much longer do I have to put up with the hours

The sleepless nights

The wall staring back at me

Piercing my head

God, how much longer do I lie here

In pools of blood and streams of tears before I can see
my sweet?

…

Goodnight

…

Try not to hurt yourself in your head.

Release.

Lies are a lot like doves

Where there is one, you'll most certainly find another.

Lovemaking.

I lie down in this room so dark

And I feel a sharp pain

Not physical but a longing pain

I feel it here in this dark room
The longing
The longing

And it's long

The distance between us

And it's long

The moments spent apart

And I tell you, it's long

The time I've wasted lying here in this dark room

Trying anything under my breath

Anything to get you here

Anything to stop the pain

Anything to light the dark room

Anything to lie down next to you

Without.

I'm the greatest thing you never had.

Remember me?

I'm the part of you that always wins

The one who digs at you

Finding every imperfection

Exploiting your weaknesses

You can sit there and cry all you want

Curse me out

Call me hateful
Call me disgusting
Call me worthless

But when you look at yourself in the mirror,

Just know I'll be there staring back at you

Because I'm part of you

And maybe I'm all of you

Good luck trying to find a reason to go on in that.

Problems.

The simplest piece of advice:

Never let them come back.

Don't.

S_A_V_E_.

The distance between us will never terminate

My unrelenting heart from loving you.

Telescopes.

The feeling of simply seeing your name

Pop up on my phone is so pleasurable

So indescribable

The look of such a perfect signature.

Names.

I've been looking for you

The girl I dreamed up

The one in my head so perfect

It's you isn't it

The way you treat me is so gentle

But so strange because I've only ever been feed
cruelty

I forgot how sweet life could taste,

You make me smile and laugh

This simple thing

None of the others could pull it off.

New Glasses.

An orchestra of Susans

Or the perky yellow Rose

A field of dancing Daffodils

Or Orchids and their bows

A bouquet of joyous Irises

Or Tulips on the floor

A shiny new Chrysanthemum

Or Carnations at your door

I want them all in yellow

For the color is too much

I want them all in yellow

For the softness of your touch.

Marigolds.

Lord I love her smile,

What I wouldn't give to make that smile

The first thing I see every morning.

Awaken.

There is more to a woman than her attractive figure

Here I find someone who keeps me coming back

Who's interesting inside and out.

Layers.

Black coffee

On a morning so lifeless

Dry, empty, and dark

The sun has not yet peaked her head over

The cold blue mountains

The wind has not yet whistled her fabled good
morning

Lights red to green to yellow control the night

They alone can not break the ebony sky to dawn

But black coffee

She has the power, the only one awake

She keeps me busy

Keeps me from going back to those painful nightmares without you.

Early Worm.

The precision of each visit as it fractures the target
on my beating heart

Into hunks and scraps of awe-inspiring emotion
proves to me that you know what you're doing.

Annie Oakley.

Take my hands and use them at your disposal

Allow me to touch the peaks and river banks on your body

Make me dip my finger tips into your amorous valleys so perfectly

Cultivated on the framework of you

The landscape of your universe has always felt like polished stones

And furnished furs from far off lands

Where men would risk their lives everyday just to have a taste of what you produce

So take my hands

Place them in the center of all creation

Grant them life in your home

Permit my tongue a mouthful of what I crave

The raw honey of existence

Make us intimate

Make us forever.

Fountain of Youth.

You will come around one of these dreary long days

And I will be here waiting for our hearts to ignite.

Virtuous.

You make me smile like the sun will never set

Our love a constant

Our happiness eternal.

Cute.

You get me like no other

How you know just what to say

You have felt my pain before

Felt it from your past

Do not be afraid my dear

We can start again

Just the two of us

And be lonely no longer.

My Half.

The sea is so vast

Fish from the deep both majestic and wild

But I cast at the same hole

Knowing only this one

Is unrivaled in beauty

Fisherman.

Forbidden is our love as we converse in secret

The moistening of lips through the phone

The perfect pauses in place

Creating the idea we both wish to exploit

Next time we met when he is out of town.

Visit.

I'm addicted to you

The way you flash your eyes at me

The way you brush your hair

How sweet you are

Always apologizing for nothing

It's incredibly cute, just like your voice

Which is nothing short of music

Everything about you is all so beautiful

And I'm addicted to every part of you,

I want a piece of everything.

Injection.

Flashing through my veins

You ignite my beating heart

In toxic burns of passion

Nothing short of being sinfully delicious.

White.

The heat of her mouth

So close to mine

The moisten walls within this place

The rolling tides of desire control my head

My thoughts leak with obsession

Let me in this world

Let me in.

Dehydrated.

How can a goddess claim to love a mortal man?

You don't understand how much I wish to tell you

I need to tell you

If only you knew how much I care

If only you knew how much I feel

You have my heart in shambles

I desire your touch, your voice

Your presence itself, that's all I need

If only I could tell you how I feel

To tell you what you truly mean to me.

Thoughts.

Calm the raging tides of my heart

Sail us to the edge of paradise.

Tides.

I know you well enough to understand

I understand that you're hard on yourself

One day you're going to open those marble green eyes of yours

See the strong survivor of a woman

The embodiment of force

Accept your faults with grace

And spread your wings, taking off.

Fly.

This veil of benevolence cannot hold the creature

That gargles and mumbles beneath it

You are wise to avoid the nasty speech and aroma

It tries to lore you in,

Only to reveal falsehoods to you

It judges your every move with its ancient eyes

Just know that this monster is blind to the real you

What it names you is groundless.

Shroud.

Her name rolls off the tongue effortlessly

More so than the taste she leaves lingering

Coating the walls of my mouth in a passionate
obsession

Like no other.

36 Heart.

This woman is fierce like rolling thunder

She whispers to the wild

Trees crumble to the ground

Lightning strikes sporadically

She can cause a beautiful anarchy

Where there shall be no disorder

She cast her image upon my flesh

Sparks- ignition

I want to keep this moment

This burst of impulsive desire

The feeling of volts, bolts, and jolts along my skin

When she moves her hands like current down my
chest

It fuels me with a delicate flicker

I live to become like her

Fiery, chaotic, a beautiful disaster

A force of nature

A perfect imitation

The final product of life

Love limitless.

Entropy.

My heart is a diamond

You are its jeweler

Be slow and graceful as you cut away the black

And make me your perfect prize,

Beauty is in fact in the eye of the beholder.

Brilliant.

Nothing is more admirable than who you are

How you carry yourself from all the worries,
bad luck, false judgments, and past mistakes that
overwhelms your soul

The weight of you would crush city after city

Yet you find a way to pass by with grace

You step to impress and impress you do

Because no one you pass could hold the weight like
you.

Acceptance.

I'll tell you,

She is a model of perfection

She never has to try to be beautiful

There's honestly nothing she does that's unattractive

And from me to you

I think she looks the best when she's in her sweats.

Natural.

Under our breaths or under our covers

It's so easy to find

The difference between us.

Attract.

I may not have the best diction

Or all the right words to say

I may stumble and fall on phrases

And make you turn away

The only thing I'm good at

Is trying with all my heart

To let you know you're beautiful

All of you, a work of art.

A Lover's Verse.

Hold my hand

Guide me through the midnight sky

A sea of ebony and rose and lavender

Mixed intimately throughout our screen

It may be dark

We may be dark

But if there's one thing I've learned it's that

You can be dark and yet beautiful

When I'm with you

We're beautiful even without the sun.

Eclipsio.

It's amazing how quickly I've found myself

falling for you.

Eyes of ocean and evergreen

Leave goosebumps upon my skin

Hills of flesh baring constant

Remembrance to her gorgeous

This girl so pure and lovely,

How do I make her mine?

Permanence.

Wow

Just wow

That's all that runs through my head when I'm with
her

She has that voice so tender and comforting

It's unlike anything I've ever known

She laughs and smiles without force

I love that she is real

I love that she is genuine

The way she makes me feel this happiness

Something I've never felt before.

It's A Whole New World Out There.

Let these fingers ride down your divide

Collecting the sap that sticks so easily

As I wipe you clean of your past

And fill you with your future.

Territorial.

After all you do for him

And he pays you with hurt instead of happiness

Look for someone who can give instead of take

There are people out there who love

They are closer than you believe

They deserve your attention

Just as you deserve theirs.

Better.

It's a beautiful thing

When you find your reflection talking back to you.

Mirrors.

The longer we lay here in the pools of kindness and
tenderness
nestled in your heart

The greater my desire radiates to be more

Lust will whisper her brainwashing hymns
commanding me to speak

We're just playing around

Then our eyes lock at the presence of each other

Once you give me the look I'll know it's true,

I want you

So let's be more.

Fornication.

When I close my eyes to fall asleep

I dream of you, I dream of us

Every night I welcome these dreams because nothing
is better

Than spending the night with you.

Bedtime.

Her eyes are full moons each eclipsing my heart

I beg for more by first the bed of her tongue

Then the moist love of her lips brushing the temple of
my world

She penetrates this place relentlessly

As we exchange tastes of worlds far and vast

She has my sun there, and I see only a horizon

The light of her warm, inviting heart starts a new day
within me

She starts a new life with me

With this sunrise please continue to bring your
foreign goods

Bring them to the harbor of my mouth

The home of my hungry taste buds

That scream your name

They scream your name
They scream your name.

Looks.

I may not accompany my love during all her travels

And it might be impossible for me to experience all the fun

But as long as she's happy

As long as she is enjoying her time

That's all I need from her.

Distance.

I could spend an eternity in those eyes.

Golden rays or crimson peaks

Emerald cities to deep blue seas

The autumnal colors, falling leaves

None of life's phenomenal scenes

Compare to that of my beautiful queen.

Portrait.

Dive into her, head first

A spring of caramel wonderland

Salty, sweet, and sticky

Mouth watering goodies and clouds of marshmallow

She's candy, my sugar

Sweeter than life itself

More desirable than anything

I wish to lay in her honey hole

Live with crystals so sweet upon my skin

Shiny like gems in glass so candied.

Gum.

We could so easily be more than friends

And effortlessly be more than lovers.

Royalty.

Be strong enough to make decisions

Not for the sake of other's feelings

But do what you believe is right

Your happiness depends on it.

Mission.

Waiting for you to see what you're missing.

How long do you plan on acting like it's not there

Our spark

Our connection

Let's cut the games and plug up.

Power-Saver Mode.

They all support me in my recovery

From the addiction you lead me to depend on

Every second of every breath

When I begged to have a look inside your demented mind

Or when I craved a taste of that silky-smooth skin of yours

All of which did more harm than good to a junkie like me.

Rehabilitation.

Your sun-kissed smile will fill the whole room

With passion and hopes of a better tomorrow.

Fortune.

You are my world

It's your gravity that keeps me centered

The rivers and streams

The mountains and valleys

All breathtaking

Your radiant flowers blossom in my presence

They keep me dilated and smiling,

Prepared to explore this new terrain

Every inch and every pore

Dive deep into the caves that hold your darkest
secrets

Secrets only I will uncover

Secrets known only to me

This marvelous masterpiece of world

I will settle it's every grain of sand

And every blade of grass

Leaving no stone unturned.

Planetary.

What do I need to do to be prescribed to you.

Do you notice how much I desire your company

How I long to be more

To include you in my intimate world

The only world where I can finally give you the
feeling of pleasure

That has fled you so long ago,

You deserve someone who will put you before
themselves

You deserve to be happy.

Principle of Proximity.

To whom it may concern,

I want you to know the truth

I love you

Even more than you already know

But it's difficult for me

Because I am chasing a woman so bound to another

However, this should come as no surprise to you

You know how phenomenal you are

How attractive you can be

You shape monuments, sculptures in my heart

For you are the only one who has ever built within me

Instead of level anything I carried around

This is how I came to want you

This is how I know I need you.

Architect.

Her beauty is more than a figure with curves

No, her strength is what I find all the more stunning.

Phoenix.

Will you wait for me?

While he takes your hand and uses you

Less of love and more of a lustful desire indoctrinated into our youth

How he promises to always love you

How he promises to follow up on his word, but never seems to...

He calls to complain

Bitch you out over the phone because you did nothing but love him

Yet you see you've pissed him off

Will you wait for me?

Because I will wait for you

I will wait till he breaks your pretty little heart

I will fix his mistakes

I will be the glue to make you whole again.

Fixer.

I'm here for you

I'll always be here for you

Where is he?

Fluff.

Pretty young thing put on me

Grip tight

Let our bodies talk

Make new discoveries

Find the parts of us hypnotically immaculate.

Buried.

The memories of you are being overwritten

By my sweetest inamorata

Who is superior to you in every way imaginable
Inamorata...unique enough to describe her.

Florescence.

She walks in earth shattering steps

Even the ground gives up to her.

Crater.

Picking and picking at this wall you've constructed

I'm trying so hard for you

You know I'm always here for you

Has this paradigm locked me out

Keeping me secluded from more

Oh how I dread the thought

Oh how I dread losing you

Handed over to a nobody,

A boy who will treat you like an instrument for sex

A trophy for his less than impressive company

Yet here I am for you

Still trying for you

I crave this love of yours like a fire so passionate

Picking away at this wall

Hoping one day to make a dent

Hoping one day you'll open your eyes

Hoping one day you'll see who really cares

Welcome.

To be so consumed by lust and manipulation

That you turn your backs on the only ones
who ever gave a damn about you

Is troubling...

Not only for them but for me,

How could I have been so focused on pacifying this
demon

That I left my army of angels warming benches in my
absence.

This is to my day-ones

Thank you for everything

I hope you can forgive me.

Re-acceptance.

I miss your voice,

God I want to hear that voice

That song

All the highs and all the lows

I want to hear you sing it to me

Tell me what I do that drives you mad

Tell me what I do that makes you want me

What do I do that gives you joy

Tell me

And tell me what more I can do to make you mine
forever

Sing it to me.

Voice.

It's so cold without you here.

Help me burn away the pain

Fueled by your fiery passion to ignite

Let us scorch our bonds to ash

Our spark to catalyze

Our cyclone of deliverance.

Fields.

I want to be sure you understand, my love

I'll never harm you

I'll never judge you, belittle you

Never fear, my love

I'll always be there for you.

Here.

He will never know

How I lay here planning to take his sweet little thing

Into my arms and never let go.

Conquer.

Don't let her fight her demons alone

Be the sword that pierces their hearts

The shield that shatters their menace

But most of all,

Be the wings that lift her up.

Un-depress.

Running will do you no good

I will hunt you my prey

Through valleys of fire and storms of ice

And when I get my hands on you, you will be mine

You will be captive to my love

A forceful feeling of being whole

You'll feel it, you'll take it

My love, it will keep you safe

You'll hunger for more

And then you and I will have peace

Locked in cages for the rest of forever

In darkness which binds us close

Touching, clinging, molding into one another

You'll be mine and you will feel love.

Syndromic.

If you assess the situation long enough

You'll know that we are strong enough now

To become anything, we desire.

Grew.

Bend her over with more than just drinks and empty
compliments

Her body should be picked apart piece by piece

Individually admired

From her gorgeous strands of hair

To her perfectly short toes that dance independently

When she tries to hide how much she loves those
dirty songs
you put on her playlist

Those songs remind her of you

How much she truly loves you

So if anything, please love her back

Listen to her problems, her stories, her dreams

Don't use her as your putty to mold and abuse

She's so much more than that

She's courageous, stunning, and intelligent

Most importantly she's a queen

So treat her as such

She already thinks you're a king.

Crowned.

There's so much of you

Layers beneath that golden body
Tell me more

I lose myself in the beating of your heart

Your hypnotic voice

Yes, the one I've grown so accustomed too

How you shine like diamonds or better yet the stars

Your eyes like fireworks softly raining on my mind

Do I dare say more?

You flood me with every part of you

And I must say,
It's always sunny with you by my side.

Promise Me You'll Stay.

What do you dream about when you put your sweet

little head to rest?

The sun never shines

The flowers never bloom

The birds never chirp

There's nothing without you

God, how I miss you

What's the point of waking up in a bed without you
here?

The only place I dare to dream is an island of just me
and you

Here I'll feel the sun's rays

Smell the roses in the morning

Whistle birds to sleep

And lay my head next to yours

Our toes buried deep in the sand

A tide carrying away all our fears

We'll simply be happy

We'll be forever

Just you and me on an island I like to call Paradise.

Paradise.

To start over with you and begin anew

Do it right this time

You may have concerns, but I can debunk them all

Because with determination like mine,

Nothing can slow me down from loving you

With all my heart.

Character.

There's a boy out there who can't help but see heaven

in your eyes.

The most beautiful girl I've ever laid eyes on

So naturally perfect

Soft and gentle, but with an edge and a contagious smile

That lights up my whole world

How I wish to stay with her

Stay with her while she strikes a pose

Wearing her cute little pajamas

While she sings a song, probably loud and heavy

While she plays with makeup

While she rants about her work

While she tells her secrets

I want to be there with her for it all

I want to get to know her, this I am certain.

Hallway.

Time can heal hearts but it will not give you peace

A level head comes when you decide to free yourself

Free yourself from the shackles that have been haunting you.

Lessons.

I'm afraid of your beauty

It's unlike anything I've ever seen

It burns into me

Please free me from this torture,

Days go by and my skin is pierced by bone

I spit out the pain as blood

Hoping that something will stick to these pages

Something to leave a remembrance of us

You have no idea,

The longing,

The obsession of wanting a love like yours

On rainy days like this

You by my side on the autumnal sidewalk

Both wet from weather

Wet from our experiences

Drenched in sludge of our past

Both close…yet so far apart

Rest in me- the rain with you and me

Blind me with more than beautiful

Blind me with love that will cauterize the pain.

Rain.

You are the butterflies that dance in my heart

Singing heavenly songs and shaping new art

Their golden tipped wings leak tears from the moon

The only witness that night, awaited kiss to a swoon.
And the butterflies fly away...

Garden.

It becomes too difficult, describing your elegance
Words cannot hold you high enough
So to let you know you're beautiful both inside and
out
A journey to your deepest parts I must undertake
Flawless actions and executions of our plans outlined
in sheets
Speak to levels known only to partners of immense
intimacy
Your walls produce music that echoes throughout my
mind
The delicious sounds of us as you scream in
understanding-
Knowing this, this is how beautiful I think you are.

Actions.

Is friendship the peak

Our relationship more molehill than mountain

Or are you as daring as I to take part in this
expedition

Climbing in elevation

Getting to know the better parts between us

A view so gorgeous and breathtaking.

View.

Blind by eyes entrancing- irresistible

While mesmerized by a smile so lustrous

You're the magnet for my longing heart.

34 Heart.

Give me your heart and I will give you the world.

Dreams of lips locked between us

Hands running through your hair

Endless eyes of ocean blue

You have me stop and stare

My number one, my everything

A landscape divine

I'll offer up my heart to you

You'll be forever mine.

Wish.

Your voice is music to my ears

An entrancing melody with increasing pitch

You get excited, the smile radiates your face

The way your eyes lock to me

Focusing

Checking to see if I'm really there

Talking to me

Staying by my side

Just keep talking girl

Do this for the rest of forever.

Coffee Date.

She's strong and she supports me.

Why ask for anything more?

They crash into my walls

Brick by brick

A stone fortress to moonlit sand

It's you

The one who flooded my heart

Dismantled me

Drowned me in love

Pulled me deeper and deeper into the abyss of your dreams

Dreams of sunsets

Walks on the beach

A dimly lit boardwalk,

The perfect place to make a move

Eyes outline your body

A body of sun-kissed glass

A body glazed in summer salts

The body whose waves penetrate

Brick by brick

Melting- eroding my barricades

It's no use

I fall to my knees every time

I crumble like a stone

Like stone I'm crushed to sand.

Boardwalk.

It's simple,

I dream of us playing in the snow

Pointing to the stars

Taking photographs to capture each moment

They'll last forever

They'll tell of all our crazy adventures

Everything we get ourselves into

And baby, all I could ever ask is to spend my life by your side

Taking these pictures

Capturing these moments

Loving you every step of the way.

Polaroid.

My words will never do her justice

Like the dust that falls from shooting stars

Or the pigment change in autumn

The vibrant glow of rainbows

A fan of peacock's feathers

Bouquets of rosy valentines

Hugs from distant relatives

Alluring sounds of silver bells

Or simply Merry Christmas

Flowers that bloom after winter storms

Balloons at children's parties

Good Word received on Sunday mornings

And kisses to you, goodnight

There are no words to let you know

She embodies all things beautiful

Joyous, pure, breathtaking

She's my nebula never fading.

Nebula.

Your golden smile…if only I could put it to words.

I will never hold you back

I will never keep you from reaching your dreams

I will push you to succeed

I will lift you to the stars.

Affirmations.

Page by page

I want to immerse myself in you

And like a good book I'll never put you down

Every part of you is so rich and captivating

I dare to turn another page

Seeing more and more of you fully illustrated in
vibrant colors,

Jaw-dropping figure, and hypnotic eyes,

I press on scanning every word

Learning your loves
Learning your hates
Learning things that make you giggle
And things that make you sob

I lose track of time within you

So focused in on what could come next

You're more than just beautiful
You're more than just interesting
You're a masterpiece

Page by page

You become my favorite read.

Pages.

How warm it must be to hold you,

The Sun herself

Giving life

Giving love

Giving everything to her dearly devoted.

Snug.

You watch her worry

She struggles with herself

But you know the power in her bones

You know that she will overcome her trials

She always does.
And it's stunning.

Struggles.

You're my lamp of hope shining rays of brilliance

The only light in my life to uncover and burn away

All the darkness I've been plagued with for so long.

Bulb.

Radiant beauty, candied eyes

More gorgeous than a sunrise

Caring, kind, and generous too

Oh how I long to be with you

Mind a museum of masterful art

Forgot to mention that you're smart

Every inch perfect and flirtatious

Hearts beating blood, salacious

In my dreams kiss me goodnight

I'll make you happy, my sweet delight.

77 Heart.

She had enough love to save his life.

You, the young goddess from which I rest my
unworthy eyes

Why do you occupy another with your charm and
enchantment
while I gaze at you, mouth ajar leaking temptations
from my lips
cracked by both lust and thirst?

The only remedy is the savory salts that lay anxious
on your skin

Drop the axe on this former lover of yours

Swing and behead him for he failed to please you

Remove him from our presence

Cling to my body instead

I will offer you your darkest satisfactions
I will be your shepherd of concupiscence.

Salt.

To fall asleep next to you

By the heat of your mouth

Holding your hand forever.

Desire.

I may never be your first love
I won't ever be your first kiss
I missed out on your first time
And maybe even more than it

I'll never be the first at all
At anything, I can't deny
But if you count on one thing
I promise that I'll try

I'll try my best and hardest
To be your rock and home
The one you'll always count on
The one who writes you poems

I'm nothing more than human
I can't gift you any power
In fact I'm pretty much a loser
Don't think I'm being sour

The only thing I'm good at
Is loving you for you
All your problems and your messes
Are now my problems too

Let me be the one who frees you
From your troubles deep within
I may not be the most experienced
But at least just let me in

I care about your life
I care about you love
I'm not a knight in shiny armor
But at least when you look above

To see the stars in all their brilliance
How they shine for you each night
Remember that I'll be the one
The one who's here to fight

The one who will fight for you
Every day and every hour
The one who will fight for you
Even when you lose your power

I may never be the first at much
I won't ever be the first at all
But I swear on all that's holy
I'll never let you fall.

One.

I miss her,

The way she kills the air
How she freezes the moment
She births butterflies in my stomach
She causes my pores to leak sweat

I miss that

Her laugh that melts my heart
Her smile that is nothing short of contagious
Her beautiful strands of hair that get lost on us as we
stare

I miss her

If I can promise one thing
This distance will never beat us
Not when I'm involved.

Counting.

The sound of your voice

A most hypnotic song

This masterful melody

Sing it all life long
And to me it's unmatched.

Unmatched.

Give your mind a rest, exhale your lonely past.

You're so cute when you act shy

Trying to hide yourself from the world

Trust me darling,

You are more beautiful than anyone could ever imagine.

Trust.

Fake smiles are what they'll feed you

Wisdom is knowing what's real.

Experience.

My heart belongs to her

It beats in sync to her song

That alluring song of her voice

I want to hear her every morning

I want to hear her every night

Every sound she makes

My heart will beat with her.

Metronome.

My master, the screen

Day in and day out

Post

Posting

Posts

New requests

New friends

New comments

Check your fucking DMs

It's all bullshit

Are we meant to live like slaves?

Live like machines?

Texting ones and zeros

Pictures instead of words

Did we lose the ability to construct images through

language?

I can't live like this

I'd rather spend my life chasing your entrancing eyes
through sidewalks and streets
Than log hours stalking image after image
Let's talk for hours with coffee and a book
Not mercilessly text throughout the day

Let's be real

We aren't slaves to our phones

Let's get lost, you and I
And instead of posting
We'll be living.

Slave.

Dear Love,

Days feel longer and longer
The further we're apart
There's nothing more I want
Than to hear your beating heart

I know patience is a virtue
But patience is also pain
At least when I see you
You'll take away the rain

When you see me once more
Will it be like old times
Will you race me to the stairwell
Will you joke about the crimes

I want to be your always
The one whom I write
This girl is a rockstar
World's most beautiful sight

And that's what's so difficult

Being so far away

If I could have one power

I'd chose to make her stay

Be with me through this absence

I know it's not too long

I know when I get back to you

I'll feel like I belong

And if I can make one thing clear

This woman is unstoppable

A force to be reckoned with

Something I never thought possible

When the time comes to reunite

The happiest man I'll be

I'll hold you close and hug you tight

Together, you and me.

Undress more of those beautiful thoughts

Dancing circles in the meadow of your mind.

Speak To Me.

She beat me down to nothing

I chose to get up

Training

Training

Training

I'm stronger now

The part of me missing,

The part of me unable to defeat you before

I harnessed it again

Self-love.

It was never about you.

Untitled.

Moonlit skin and midnight breezes

She's radiant gold

Perfection incarnate,

Grip me close and share your power

In this hour I devote myself to thee

Allow us this moment

I've shown you my true intentions

My heart beckons to you

This angel in the night

Pure and yet seemingly provocative

Tell me you understand

This desire I desire

This hunger I hunger

Her hourglass frame has ticked and tocked the clock
of my mind into obsession

For I know she has no interest

But to me she is all that interest can be

Cutting diamonds with emerald stares and my heart
into hairs- split

Unlike her innocently chocolate linen

That makes up her lion's mane

Fierce and yet still beautiful
Even in the eyes of the prey
Especially in the eyes of the prey,

Who wish to kiss Death and her marvelous linen
mane.

Shrouded Abbey.

You cut yourself with words so harsh and false

You make an adversary out of your body and heart

The whispers of ugliness drown away the time we have left to spend together

Believe me,

You have to believe me,

Nothing the Lich of your mind tells you is true

You are amazing

Everyone can see your beauty

Everyone can see your courage

Everyone will see you as I see you

And I know you're stunning.

Worst Enemy.

My girl is more than just rainbows

And sunshine

And candied rose meadows

Or glitter bombed presents

A world so fiery- luminescent

She's also my midnight

A both mystical and dark

A sheen of ebony, onyx

And permanent black mark

Her shyness

Her longing

A beautiful loneliness

Her loneliness no longer

For our bond has grown stronger.

And she will share this world with me.

Midnight.

Her breath could level cities.

I wrote this for you

I want you to be happy

Smile for me

Breathe for me

Everything will work itself out

You have to believe that

You have to believe me

Promise me and smile while you can

The world is nothing without you

You alone have this power to light up the life of those

around you

Grow gardens in the hearts of us

And lay us all to rest with a kiss goodnight.

I Know.

Nothing is more beautiful then how she dances at midnight

She spins and spins and spins

All the while singing heavy metal or rapping her favorite artists

And it's so cute to watch

Especially when she misses a beat or confuses a verse

Maybe she'll just make up her own lyrics

It's so wonderful when she's free to be herself

Free from judgement

Free from the world

And every part of it is amazing.

Socks.

Running my palms over marbles

Exploring this infamous masterpiece

Clutching your passion hand in hand

The taste of your sugar cane blood still leaks

From my fretting tongue

Drip

Drop

Call it infatuation

Call it obsessive

Give me everything you have to offer

We are so close now, admit it

Don't try to neglect us

Let the rest of them fade into your past

I'm here now, *that's all that matters*

You think about it too

O U R   B O N D

It's more than magnetic

Awaken my eyes to a rebirth of everlasting bliss and color.

Siren.

I just want to warm your heart

Cause your smiles

Give you everything I can give to make you happy.

Christmas.

You are the best part of everyday.

It's a wonderland of ecstasy or a wasteland of love

When you speak words to me

Melting my heart into a creamy milk chocolatey
syrup

So sticky and gooey and addictive

A flavor I share only with you as you dip your tiny
little hands
into my hollow valves

Contracting with every breath

Every touch

Giving rise to pumps and pumps

Bloody and sinful

So delightfully devilish

Especially after you put those sweet salty fingers
coated
in my candied love

All over your tongue, spread like a frosted glaze with
moans
from each and every taste bud sucking the life from
your tips

Extracting every drop of me

Your tongue strangles the treat

Then you'll understand what it truly means to be
worshipped.

Chocolate Hearts.

Shower me in the waterfall of your brilliant blue eyes

Every drop exciting my skin to a higher heaven

Hairs stand up and bow their heads to you as if to
praise
your holiness for giving them life once more

Keep me submerged in you

Keep me down, drowning me in your love

Feed me, bath me, hold me

I will drink from you

Till death do us part.

Earthly.

Those thoughts that plague your mind
Are anything but true
You're nothing like you see yourself
There's no one quite like you

You fight those pesky demons
The ones that haunt your heart
Don't let them get the best of you
You've been perfect from the start

And if you don't believe me
Then let me offer this
I've never seen a stronger woman
My everlasting bliss

Doubtful.

My blood will scorch your name on my heart.

Stars are pretty and all

But you're so much more than something that can
burn out
in the blink of an eye, no

Your light, your love

That shit is undying.

No Comparison.

This is yours

All of it

Every tear shed
Every eye dilated
Every laugh shared
This is it...

Humanity in print

We make mistakes
And that's a fact
We make many mistakes
But to learn from them
To become better
To forgive and forget
That's what is important
That's what's strong

If there is one certainty

If there is one thing I didn't mess up

Probably the only thing I've done right, is you

Yes, you

You, the most important thing to me

All of this is yours

Own it and wear it

Love it

Take care of the words

You're special to me

You are anything but a mistake.

Thank you for everything,

I couldn't have done it without you.

98630614R00171